The *Financially Informed* Boomer

7 Rules to Help Boomers
Achieve a Secure Retirement

JIM E. SLOAN

Written and Published by Jim E. Sloan

Cover Design by Cathi Stevenson
www.bookcoverexpress.com

Printed by LightningSource.com

Investment Advisory Services offered through Global Financial Private Capital, LLC, an SEC Registered Investment Advisor.

Table of Contents

Disclaimer..*v*

Foreword..*vii*

Rule #1
Know When To Begin Your Social Security Benefits 1

Rule #2
Know The Investments You Own 11

Rule #3
Creating a Lifetime Paycheck 25

Rule #4
Have a Plan When Your Health Fails 35

Rule #5
Avoid These Two Potential Costly IRA Mistakes...........47

Rule #6
Get a Basic Estate Plan In Order.......................................55

Rule #7
Know the Difference Between a Broker
and an Advisor. 65

About the Author..*69*

Disclaimer

This book is intended for educational purposes only and was written to provide accurate and authoritative information regarding the subject matter covered. While the author has used his best effort in writing this book, please understand that even accurate information can become outdated quickly as the IRS and Congress routinely change the rules and regulations pertaining to these issues.

The author is not engaged in rendering legal or tax advice. If you require such advice, you are encouraged to seek qualified tax or legal counsel for your particular situation. The author and publisher are not liable or responsible to any person or entity who suffers any loss or damage caused or alleged to be caused directly or indirectly by the information contained in this book.

Foreword

Over the years of helping boomers improve their financial circumstances, I have uncovered multiple areas of concern that have the potential to derail the retirement dreams of many boomers. This book attempts to help boomers understand some of the financial landmines that exist and how to try to safely navigate around them.

I don't believe anyone has a monopoly on good ideas. I do believe that every boomer should seek wisdom and counsel and get a second opinion on their current financial path. The second opinion will do one of two things for you. It will validate that the path you're on is leading you to where you want to go. Or, it will raise enough red flags that you will want to investigate your current position.

Either way, I just think it is a great idea to seek a trusted advisor and get an unvarnished view of where you are and where you're heading. You just may improve your financial circumstances along the way.

Rule #1

Know When To Begin
Your Social Security Benefits

When should you begin Social Security benefits – age 62, 66, 70 or somewhere in between? This is a question that many boomers are asking and if you guess wrong, it could be an irreversible mistake that may cost you many thousands of dollars in lost income over your and your family's lifetime.

This chapter will help you understand the various ages you could begin receiving your Social Security benefits along with the advantages and disadvantages of each, along with five different ways that would help you increase your benefits.

Have you ever called a Social Security Administration office? Typically, you could call three days in a row, ask the same question to three different SSA employees and receive two or three different answers.

You could go to the Social Security Administration website and learn the rules for yourself and try to make an informed decision. However, typically what I have discovered is that good planning requires someone helping you understand the long-term consequences of the decisions that you make today. There is no one-size-fits-all answer as to when you should begin collecting your benefits. It depends on your particular situation.

For example, someone beginning early benefits at age 62 and living into their 90's, could end up leaving hundreds of thousands of dollars on the table. However, it may make sense for some to claim early benefits if they are not working and have limited resources. On the other hand, if someone is still working, claiming early benefits may not be best for them because they may lose some or all of their benefits until they attain full retirement age.

For many years, I have asked countless boomers, "When do you plan to begin Social Security benefits?" What I have found is that many boomers either don't know or just guess, based on the experiences of relatives, friends or co-workers. And, in the past few years, many have told me that they think they should begin at age 62 because Social Security may not be there and they want to get all they can now. Very few have ever done the math. As I mentioned earlier, making this mistake may cause some to lose a large portion of their nest egg over their and their family's lifetime.

The best way to determine when you should begin your Social Security benefits is to have a trusted advisor review your particular situation, run several what-if calculations and compare those numbers to your particular situation. Only then, can you make an informed decision.

You could go to the SSA website and run calculations for yourself on how much you'll receive and at what age. However, that is just the starting point.

Knowing the answers to the following questions will help you make an informed decision as to when you should begin collecting your Social Security benefits;

1) Other than SSI, what other sources of income will you have and where will it coming from?

2) How much of the other income is taxable?

3) How much do you have in savings and investments?

4) Are you working now, and if so, when do you want to retire?

5) Are you married, and if so, when will your spouse be retiring?

6) If married, is your spouse retired or retiring from the Texas Teacher Retirement System?

7) How is your health and do you have longevity in your family?

There are additional questions, but you get the idea. This information is necessary to help you and your spouse, if married, make informed decisions and maximize your Social Security benefits.

Are there ways to increase your Social Security benefits?

Yes there are, but before we address five different ways to accomplish this, let's review a highly discussed but rarely implemented strategy that the government just shut down. It is called the *repay and reapply strategy.*[1]

---

1   http://www.federalregister.gov/articles/2010/12/08/2010-30868/amendments-to-regulations-regarding-withdrawal-of-applications-and-voluntary-suspension-of-benefits

Until recently, Social Security recipients could legally stop their monthly checks, repay previously received income with a lump sum payment and reapply for a higher monthly benefit. Since there was no interest charged on the repaid benefits, those who took advantage of this option ended up receiving an interest-free loan from the government and always had the option to repay and restart at the higher benefit amount later, if circumstances dictated.

This strategy became more popular as retirees sought out prudent methods to boost income during a near-zero interest rate environment.

With little advance notice and less fanfare, on December 8, 2010, the Social Security Administration announced that "effective immediately" the opportunity to repay and reapply for retirement benefits would be severely curtailed.

In restricting the activity, the SSA cited the interest-free repayments as being a significant cost to the Trust Fund, as well as the amount of paperwork and personnel hours required to process a withdrawal and subsequent restarting of the benefits.

Now those who wish to *repay and reapply* must do so within 12 months of originally beginning their retirement benefits, and can only perform the tactic once, rather than the unlimited number of repeats recipients could previously perform.

The closing of this loophole may be understandable, but it adds one more layer of urgency to the informed decision of when boomers should begin collecting their Social Security benefits.

Even without this strategy, there are five ways you might increase your Social Security benefits[2].

1) Work longer, earn more.

Your earnings record for Social Security continues to be updated as long as you work and pay into Social Security. If you keep working at a relatively high salary, it can cause one of your lower-earning years to drop off the 35-year earnings record and serve to boost your primary insurance amount (PIA). This advice is especially important for people who do not have 35 years of high earnings, such as women who have stayed home with their children. It even applies to high-earners in their 50s and 60s; although the earnings in their early years are indexed for inflation, the indexed amount is likely lower than their current salary. For example, after indexing, the maximum wage base of $10,800 in 1973 counts as about $55,000. So a person who already has 35 years of maximum earnings can continue to improve their earnings record by replacing one or more of those early indexed years with today's higher earnings.

2) Delay applying for benefits.

After attaining full retirement age, if your situation dictates that you should delay receiving SSI benefits, your benefit would increase by 8% annually until age 70, at which time, you are required to begin collecting benefits. In a low-return environment, those 8% annual delayed credits that an unclaimed benefit earns between the ages of 66 and 70, could end up being extremely valuable. Most people consider their 'break-even age' or the age at

---

2   www.ssa.gov, Elaine Floyd, Savvy Social Security Planning

which the cumulative total under the later-claiming scenario catches up to the earlier-claiming scenario. But this usually leads to earlier claiming behavior because people don't want to start out 'behind'. A better way to look at it is to consider the relative income in your old age, when you are 85 or 90. For example, the age-85 benefit for a maximum earner born in 1946 will be $3,320 if he or she applies at 62 vs. $5,844 if he or she applies at age 70, assuming 2.8% annual COLAs. The bigger risk for baby boomers is not dying too soon and leaving money on the table; it's living too long and having insufficient income in your later years when you really need it.

3) Coordinate spousal benefits.

There is a lot married couples can do to maximize their joint Social Security income, but they have to pay attention to the rules. For example, a high-earning husband can collect a spousal benefit off his wife's record between the ages of 66 and 70 while his own benefit earns delayed credits. Knowledge of the rules is essential. In order for it to work, three things must happen: 1) the wife must have applied for benefits on her own record (and if she is under full retirement age this may not be the best move); 2) the husband must not do this before he is full retirement age; and 3) when he goes to the SSA office he must tell them he wants to restrict his application to his spousal benefit (otherwise they will pay him his own benefit and all delayed credits will stop). There are too many spousal strategies to talk about here, but the main point is that you have to take into account each spouse's age and primary insurance amount (PIA) and you have to know the rules in order to implement them properly.

4) Maximize survivor benefits.

A large benefit of Social Security is that if one spouse dies, the other spouse may jump up to that spouse's benefit if it is higher. Hypothetically, let's say Jack (not a real person) dies while receiving a benefit of $2,200 a month, Jill, his wife (not a real person) can trade in her $1,100 benefit for Jack's $2,200, and this becomes her new survivor benefit. The main way to maximize the survivor benefit is to have the high earner delay benefits to age 70. This will maximize their joint income while both spouses are alive, and it will maximize the surviving spouse's income after one spouse dies. Would he rather leave Jill a monthly benefit of $3,320 or $5,844? He can ensure the higher survivor benefit for her by applying for his own benefit at 70. One important thing we've found is that applying before full retirement age is the worst thing a high earner can do, even if he is not expected to live very long. Let's say Jack applies for Social Security at 62 and dies after receiving one check. In this case Jill's survivor benefit will be based on Jack's age-62 benefit. But if he dies without having applied for Social Security, her survivor benefit would be based on his age-66 benefit, which would be about 25% higher.

5) Keep more of your Social Security income by reducing or eliminating federal taxation.

Let's discuss how much of your benefits will be subject to taxation and then learn about a strategy for some to reduce or eliminate the taxation of their Social Security benefits altogether.

Once you begin receiving your Social Security income, you will fall into one of three categories of taxation -

either none of your benefits will be taxed, 50% will be taxed or 85% will be taxed.

The amount of Social Security benefits that becomes taxable depends on how much "provisional income" you have for the year. To calculate your provisional income, start with your adjusted gross income, or AGI, which is the amount that appears on the last line on Page 1 of your Form 1040. However, don't count any Social Security benefits when figuring your AGI. Next, take the AGI number and add half of your Social Security income plus all of tax-free municipal bond income. Add all of this up and that is your 'provisional income' for the year.

0% Taxable
If your provisional income is $32,000 or less, and you file a joint Form 1040 with your spouse, your Social Security benefits will be totally federal-income-tax-free.

50% Taxable
If your provisional income is between $32,001 and $44,000, and you file a joint Form 1040 with your spouse, you must report up to 50% of your Social Security benefits as income on your Form 1040.

If your provisional income is between $25,001 and $34,000, and you file single or head of household, you must report up to 50% of your Social Security benefits as income.

85% Taxable
If your provisional income is above $44,000, and you file a joint Form 1040 with your spouse, you must report up to 85% of your Social Security benefits as income on your Form 1040.

If your provisional income is above $34,000, and you do not file jointly, the general rule is that you must report up to 85% of your Social Security benefits as income on your Form 1040.

Can you reduce or eliminate Social Security taxation altogether?

In many instances, I have seen where a taxpayer can reduce their provisional income to the point where their SSI is taxed slightly or not at all.

This strategy is best used with after-tax accounts (non-retirement accounts). If your investment income is derived from IRAs, then that income is generally 100% taxable. However, if your income is derived from after-tax accounts, then only the interest earnings are taxable. So, you could potentially receive the same amount of income but only a very small percentage of the income would be taxable (interest earnings). By doing this, your provisional income is reduced to below the threshold at which your Social Security income is completely tax-free.

When should you begin receiving your Social Security benefits?

To determine the best age for you to begin your Social Security benefits, it is recommended that you seek a trusted advisor that will take the time to understand your particular situation and run the necessary calculations. Only then, will you have the information to make an informed decision.

Rule #2

Know The Investments You Own

Since entering the financial services industry in the mid-1990s, one of the biggest surprises I've found is that the majority of investors I have personally advised do not know the fees they're paying for the investments they own.

During speaking engagements, I'll ask a room full of boomers, By a show of hands, how many of you know the total fees you're paying to own your investments?" Occasionally, one or two will raise their hand. The majority tell me that they "don't know" or that they are "paying very little."

Why would an investor not know? Is this information important? Is it possible that their broker told them, but they forgot? Where can they get this information? The truth is, almost all investment statements I have seen over the years, do not report the investment fees.

The fees and expenses are reported in the prospectus for that particular investment, however, because many prospectuses are hundreds of pages long and filled with small print and legalese, the majority of people never bother to read them.

I believe every boomer should know the fees that they're paying, because over time, these fees can add up to some very hefty sums, and they are withdrawn directly from your investment accounts, whether or not your portfolio increases or decreases in value.

During my discovery meetings with prospective clients, I've routinely seen where boomers are paying 2%-3.5% per year in total fees and their portfolios are less than they were ten years ago. Someone has made a lot of money over the past ten years, but it wasn't the majority of the boomers I've met with!

For example, if you have $250,000 invested and are paying 3% per year in fees, you're paying $6,000 annually to the brokers, brokerage firms, mutual funds or variable annuity company. Then, multiply $6,000 per year by ten years and you get the picture of why it may be important to know how much in fees you're paying.

To be fair, I am not against a firm charging fees to manage their clients assets. My firm charges fees and we are a transparent and full disclosure firm. I am just against a firm charging fees and not disclosing them in a manner that enables the client to understand he or she is paying.

I am writing this book in the summer of 2011 and The Wall Street Journal calls the past ten years, *The Lost Decade of Stock Investing.*[3] It is has been common to see many investors earn nothing in the past decade, but pay tens of thousands, if not hundreds of thousands of dollars in total fees. When I say total fees, I mean the total of the disclosed and undisclosed fees. When it comes to mutual funds, there are disclosed and undisclosed fees. In fact, the Wall Street Journal ran an article in March 2010 titled, *The Hidden Costs of Mutual*

---

3   The Wall Street Journal, David Weidner, October 15, 2009

Funds.[4] The subtitle for that article was *Portfolio managers can rack up steep expenses buying and selling securities, but that burden isn't reflected in a fund's standard expense ratio.*

An investor could go to a third party research company such as www.morningstar.com and input their mutual fund ticker symbol and get the disclosed fees on their particular mutual fund. But what they won't find are the undisclosed fees, which are the trading costs that the client pays for the brokerage firms to buy and sell securities.

The article goes on to quote Stephen Horan, head of professional education content and private wealth at CFA Institute, a nonprofit association of investment professionals. Mr. Horan estimates that trading costs for stock funds total 2% to 3% of assets annually, though conservative estimates place them closer to 1%. Whichever is correct, when you add the disclosed and undisclosed fees of many stock mutual funds, the fees that the investor pays may be close to 2%+ annually.

Does the performance you're receiving justify the fees you're paying?

That is a question every investor should ask themselves, and ask regularly. There are many investment choices to consider, however, if you're paying fees for money management and the investments have underperformed market averages or your portfolio is less than it was ten years ago, maybe it's time to begin interviewing for your next advisor.

From someone that meets with boomers weekly, I humbly say, "You owe it to yourself and your family".

---

4   The Wall Street Journal, Anna Prior, March 1, 2010

Now that we've discussed the fee aspect of mutual funds, let's review some other investment tools and shine a light on their associated costs.

Other Investment Vehicles

- **Stocks**

  With stock purchases and liquidations, there is a fee for buying and selling a stock position. If for example, you went to www.etrade.com, you would pay a flat fee of $9.99 to buy and sell a stock position[5] or you could do the same at www.tdameritrade.com for the same flat fee.[6]

  There are no ongoing underlying management fees unless you have an advisor managing your stock portfolio, then he or she would charge you their management or advisory fee.

- **Bonds**

  The costs to buy or sell bonds include commission costs, markups and custody fees.

  Most bond trades incur *commission costs,* which are fees that are paid to the broker who arranged a purchase or trade. Some newly issued bonds may be sold to the investor without commission costs if the issuer absorbs the commission costs; however, most trades incur commission costs. Costs can either be fixed (e.g., $15 per trade), or a percentage of the pur-

---

5   https://us.etrade.com/e/t/pricingandrates
6   http://www.tdameritrade.com/pricing.html

chase or sale amount (e.g., fifteen basis points, or .15 percent of the trade).

Markup is the difference between the price you pay for the bond and the suggested selling price.

Custody fees are fees that the brokerage house charges you to hold bonds in your account. These fees may be a specific amount for small accounts (e.g., $15 per year). For larger accounts, the custody fee may either be assessed as a specific charge per holding (e.g., eight basis points per security, or .08 percent), or a percentage of your assets (e.g., twenty-five basis points per security). [7]

- **Exchange Traded Funds**

  In general, ETFs are similar to mutual funds except that they trade intraday like stocks. They've become extremely popular because they're considered to be a "cheap" way for investors to gain exposure in the market. Before you buy, it pays to understand the true costs and how they could affect you. The costs associated with ETFs are expense ratios, commissions and bid/ask spreads.

  Expense Ratios

  Generally speaking, ETF expense ratios are lower than those of comparable mutual funds, because ETF providers don't take on the accounting in-house; nor do they include 12b-1 fees related to marketing costs, as mutual funds do.

---

7   http://personalfinance.byu.edu/?q=node/793

Commissions

In addition to trading like stocks, ETFs also carry trading commissions. The price per trade can vary by brokerage, account type, even how you order your trade (online, over the phone, etc.). Regardless, you're still subject to a flat fee with every buy and sell.

Bid/Ask Spreads

A fund's bid/ask spread is the gap between what traders are willing to pay and accept for a given ETF's shares. When trading an ETF, you purchase shares at some higher "ask" price, and sell them at a discounted "bid" price. Obviously, wider spreads will diminish returns.

For the largest, most well-traded ETFs, spreads are usually tiny; often just pennies. But for ETFs with lower assets or volume, the gap can be much wider.

Like commissions, spreads are more of a problem for frequent traders than buy-and-hold investors. But they can still wreak havoc on overall returns. [8]

I have seen investment advisory firms use ETFs as part of their client portfolios and trade ETFs for pennies on the dollar. There's an advisory management fee, but you'll know the full disclosed and undisclosed costs with these managed portfolios.

---

8 http://www.indexuniverse.com/etf-education-center/7535-understanding-the-true-costs-of-etfs.html

- **Annuities**

There are many types of annuities, but for the purpose of this book, I will share with you the three types of annuities that I have seen as most prevalent among boomers, fixed rate, fixed index and variable. All annuities are backed by the claims paying ability of the insurer and are not FDIC insured.

Fixed Rate Annuity

Fixed rate annuities are interest rate savings vehicles issued by insurance companies. They pay a locked-in interest rate for a specific term. You put your money in and then collect interest monthly or annually.

At the end of the term, you can access your principal and interest without penalties. There are no loads, sales charges or management fees. There are penalties if you get out of the contract before the term expires. And, the selling agent receives a commission from the insurer, but it does not come out of your premium.

Fixed Index Annuity

Fixed index annuities (FIA) are savings vehicles issued by insurance companies. FIAs guarantee your principal and interest as long as you fulfill the term of the contract, generally 5-15 years. Your interest is linked to a market index. Each year, if the market is positive, you get a percentage of the upside. You won't get all of the upside of the market because you are not invested in the market. However, if the market is negative, you get a 0% interest credit for that year, your principal and previously earned interest is protected and you do it all over again the next year. I've heard index annuities referred to as "safety with opportunity".

I went on the internet in May 2011 and googled *index annuity*, and found 91,600 web links…and as you know, each has their point of view, good, bad or indifferent. There are opinions out there that say index annuities are traps, scams and commission goldmines for agents. Then there are opinions out there that say index annuities do just what they are supposed to do, and that is protect your money and link your interest to the upward movement of the market without any downside risk.

Where can you go to get an objective opinion on index annuities? One of the most objective pieces I've seen on index annuities is a study conducted by the Wharton Financial Institution Center. It began with, "this study should help inform the public and correct the inaccurate information portrayed by some journalists and industry professionals."[9]

For anyone considering an index annuity, my recommendation would be to get advice from several advisors. Here's what I've found to be true, if the advisor only sells mutual funds, then he or she will spin everything against index annuities and will not offer them.

If the advisor offers index annuities only, everything will lead to an annuity sale. So, try to find an advisor that offers both securities portfolios along with

---

9   http://fic.wharton.upenn.edu/fic/Policy%20page/RealWorldReturns.pdf

annuities. Because, there are situations where one or the other, or both are appropriate. It all depends on the circumstances of each boomer. And it rarely makes sense to put all of your eggs in one basket.

FIAs use many different methods to calculate the index gains (if any) for that year. Because of the variety and complexity of the methods used to credit interest (participation rates, caps, spreads, etc.), investors should seek a trusted advisor who will help them determine if an index annuity is appropriate for their circumstances and explain in plain English how it works and what to expect.

How is my interest linked to the market?

The index-linked gain depends on the particular combination of indexing features that an FIA uses. The most common indexing features are listed below;

- **Participation Rate.** A participation rate determines how much of the gain in the index will be credited to the annuity. For example, the insurance company may set the participation rate at 80 percent, which means the annuity would only be credited with 80 percent of the gain experienced by the index.

- **Spread/Asset Fee.** Some FIAs use a spread or asset fee in addition to, or instead of, a participation rate. This percentage will be subtracted from any gain in the index linked to the annuity. For example, if the index gained 10 percent and the spread/margin/

asset fee is 3.5 percent, then the gain in the annuity would be only 6.5 percent.

- **Caps.** Many FIAs put a cap on your return. This is the maximum rate of interest the annuity will earn for that year and could change annually. For example, if the index linked to the annuity gained 10 percent and the cap rate was 8 percent, then the gain in the annuity would be 8 percent.

Expenses

It could be costly if you surrender an annuity early. FIAs are long-term investments. Getting out early may mean taking a loss. There are no up-front sales charges or fee to the consumer. FIAs have surrender penalty schedules, which decrease to 0% after a period of years outlined in the contract. The surrender penalty is assessed if the policy owner withdraws more than 10% annually. If you stay in the contract for the entire term (5–15 yrs for example), there is no surrender penalty.

Annuities give you access to 10% penalty-free withdrawals each year. And, if the policyholder were to die during the contract term, in most cases, the death benefit would be the full account value (with no surrender penalty).

Any withdrawals from tax-deferred annuities before you reach the age of 59½ are generally subject to a 10% tax penalty in addition to any gain being taxed as ordinary income. When considering a fixed index annuity, carefully read the disclosures and brochures, and insist that the agent recommending it go over this material with you, so that you can make an informed decision.

**There are tax-advantages with annuities,
but not if held inside an IRA.**

If you buy an index annuity with non-retirement money (after-tax dollars), then you will have a tax-deferred annuity and all interest earned is not taxable until you withdraw it.

If you buy an index annuity inside an IRA or retirement account, you still have the safety and guarantees of an annuity, but tax-deferral is something you already have, since retirement accounts already receive tax-deferred status.

Lifetime Income Riders

There are many Lifetime Income Riders that exist today. Essentially, it is a rider that you attach to an annuity and the rider guarantees the growth of your money for income purposes at a certain rate. There is an annual fee for this type of rider which could range from .60% to .95% annually. I've seen the guaranteed rates range from 5% to 8% annually.

Example: Let's say you bought a $100,000 index annuity and attached a 7% lifetime income rider with an annual fee of .60%. Your annuity contract will have two things going on simultaneously, the account value (AV) and the income account value (IAV). The account value (AV) is yours to control and withdraw from, and the interest is linked to the market with principal protection. Simultaneously, for income purposes, you have an income account value (IAV) that is growing at 7% annually for future income purposes. If you waited 9 years, the IAV value would double to over $200,000 for income purposes.

The policyholder could turn on the income stream in any year, but from a financial planning standpoint, it may be better to defer income from this account until needed, since it is growing at a guaranteed rate. This is assuming you have other assets to use for income while this portion of your nest egg is growing at the guaranteed rate.

Payouts could be single or joint, with joint paying out a lower amount due to the payments over two lives. Some riders offer inflation increases annually, some only when the market goes up and some not at all. There are many things to consider, so before you buy an annuity, please seek advice for your particular situation.

- **Variable Annuity**

    A variable annuity is an annuity with a range of investment options. The value of your investment will vary depending on the performance of the investment selections you make. The investment options for a variable annuity are typically mutual funds that invest in stocks, bonds, money market instruments, or some combination of the three.

    Over the past decade, I've seen the total fees associated with variable annuities range from 2.5% - 3.87% annually. On $200,000, that's $5,000 - $7,740 each year. And, that's irrespective of whether or not the account value increases or decreases.

    The total fees mentioned above are for things such as mortality and expense charges, administrative charges, rider fees, money manager fees, and a death benefit, etc. The prospectus for each variable annuity spells out the associated fees. As mentioned earlier in this chapter, the majority of boomers I've met that own variable annuities were very surprised to learn of these fees and many said "I knew I was paying something, I just didn't know it was that much" or "why wasn't I told this?".

If you're considering a variable annuity, read the prospectus carefully for fees, expenses and risk.

Variable annuities are backed by the claims paying ability of the insurer.

Search for a firm that is transparent and fully discloses this information, so that you'll know what you are paying. Be informed.

Rule #3

Creating a Lifetime Paycheck

One of the biggest challenges facing boomers is securing income streams that will last a lifetime. There has been a shift taking place for many years now, that places more responsibility on individuals to provide for themselves via savings and wealth management. Pensions are rare anymore, as many employers have shifted the retirement burden on employees by replacing their defined benefit plans (pensions) to defined contribution plans (e.g, 403b plan, 401k plan). Many employers have also eliminated or reduced the health insurance benefits for their retired employees.

This shift is occurring at a particularly challenging time for managing investments. The bear markets from 2000 to 2002 and 2007 to 2009 resulted in the worst 10-year stock market performance ever — even including the great depression.[10] The impact to the psychology of pre-retirees is likely to be long-lasting.

This chapter begins by describing the scope of America's retirement income challenge and the changes in financial thinking that boomers must make as they transition from full-time work and wealth accumulation to retirement and living off of their investments.

There are five challenges that pre-retirees face in planning for lifetime income;

---

10   Fidelity Investments; Retirement Income Planing whitepaper

- living too long

- inflation

- excessive investment fees

- too-rapid withdrawals

- rising health care costs

To improve the odds of living comfortably in retirement, boomers must develop realistic retirement income plans and cushion their investment portfolios against unforeseen financial shocks.

Aging America and the Broken Bubble

With the shift away from companies and government providing for retirement income, a majority of American households had to become first time stock market investors — directly or through their retirement savings plans. Generally, boomers are given a list of 401k investment options and told to make their selections. With greater individual responsibility comes greater risk, which was never more apparent than when U.S. equity markets experienced three down years in a row, from 2000 to 2002 or the more recent bear market from October 2007 to March 2009. These severe stock market corrections most sharply impacted people in or close to retirement and resulted in trillions of dollars of wealth being lost.

Many retirees have had to adjust their budgets and down-size expectations for retirement living. Some have had to go back to full-time work. Many people still in the workforce feel compelled to delay retirement, raise their savings, and lower their expectations about post-retirement lifestyles that had looked to be very comfortable until the market collapse in 2008.

Over the past few years, I have met pre-retirees and retirees that lost a very large portion of their nest egg. I have seen where too many investment portfolios have been decimated because of the "buy and hold" philosophy that so many brokers still recommend today. Some retirees have gone back to work in their 60's and 70's, earning minimum wage, because they had to bring in some extra income. Some pre-retirees have shed tears in my conference room after discovering the reality of not having enough assets to provide the lifetime income they thought they were going to have.

To me, the saddening part for these folks, is that it didn't have to happen. It wasn't only the market that helped derail their portfolio, it was the advice that they were given or not given that was the deciding factor in seeing half of their nest egg disappear. Most boomers I've met during the past few years that have lost half of their nest egg, in my opinion, were relying on the advice from their broker or brokerage firm, who told them something to the effect of "hang in there, it's going to come back," or "we don't want to get out now or we'll miss the ride back up," or "don't panic, everybody is going through the same thing." In my opinion, that is someone that doesn't know how to position themselves when the market is that volatile.

In fact, many boomers went through the same market volatility and maybe their nest egg decreased 6%-8% during that period. So, don't tell me that "everybody went through the same thing." That's untrue.

Entering retirement and beginning the distribution phase of one's financial life involves a major change in financial tactics, mindset and planning to successfully manage for lifetime income.

Because more of the responsibility for meeting income needs and health care expenses in retirement has shifted to boomers, it now becomes imperative to create a retirement income plan to meet your income needs for life. And if you do plan wisely, you increase the potential of enjoying your retirement years.

A 2005 study by LIMRA International, Inc., a life insurance marketing research organization, found that one in five pre-retirees had a written plan for managing assets, income, and expenses in retirement.[11]

That means 80% of pre-retirees in this study didn't have a plan at all.

New mindset

Over the years, the financial experts and brokerage firms told us to invest in stocks, bonds and mutual funds. Supposedly, over time, we could expect the stock market to return an average of 10% annually. We were told to leave it alone and over time, the ups and downs of the market would average out and we could expect a 10% annual return?

Well, that might have worked in a certain 10 year period, but it certainly hasn't worked for the past decade (2000-2010). In March 2008, *The Wall Street Journal* called this decade "The

---

11   LIMRA International, based on a 2005 survey of individuals ages 55-70 with at least $50,000 household investable assets.

Lost Decade of Stock Investing". Going forward, what can we expect from the markets and how does a boomer prepare for lifetime income streams?

Market volatility is here to stay because of the various forces at work that have a direct impact on the movement of markets. These forces are many - a nation, states and municipalities running record deficits, unfunded liabilities for Medicare, Medicaid, Social Security, the prescription drug plan and the Federal Reserve's ability to inject or withdraw money from the U.S. reserve system. When America faces large deficits, the government can print money, which leads to other concerns, mainly the devaluing of the U.S. dollar and inflation over time. When states have deficits, they can't print money, but they can layoff workers and cut benefits. When you add to this list, an unsettled world economy, terrorism and record unemployment, the markets will continue to be volatile.

How can a boomer create lifetime income streams?

One of the most common and potentially disastrous mistakes in planning for income after retirement is to base those plans on historical average returns, and then project those averages out in a linear manner for 20 years or more. This approach to planning is somewhat like deciding to wade across a river based on the average depth. The average may be four feet, but that won't help you when you're in the middle of a section that's 12 feet to the bottom. Referring to long-term averages does have some utility in the accumulation phase. It can encourage younger savers to look past short-term volatility, particularly in equities, and continue to steadily build up their assets.

In post-retirement, the options for correcting errors are more constrained. Planning retirement income streams on a linear projection of average returns can very easily create a misleading sense of security or certainty about a portfolio's chances of success. The real world of markets and investments is much more variable and unpredictable.

In my experience, over the past decade, many brokers allocated their client's nest egg amongst stocks, bonds, mutual funds and variable annuities, with the plan to leave the allocation alone and over time, it will do well and the client could begin withdrawing income each year and the portfolio would last for their lifetime because the money was going to grow at 10% annually on average. Many boomers and retirees that experienced this advice, are now having to realign their retirement dreams and goals.

Consider another approach to income planning

A simple but effective approach is to split your nest egg into several accounts and then assign job descriptions to each account. This will allow your dollars to grow or be distributed to you in the most efficient manner at all times.

Let's examine the financial picture of three twin brothers, Bob, John and Nick, all three are age 62.
(hypothetical purposes and are not real people)

Bob's Case

Bob is comfortable with a conservative level of market risk, has a $1,000,000 nest egg and is needing $40,000 in annual income. For Bob, an ideal scenario would be to invest the principal and live off of the interest. With the volatility I described earlier, can he do this and reasonably expect to achieve his goal of $40,000 annually without touching the principal? It's possible, if he finds a money manager that takes conservative risks and seeks to avoid excessive declines. There are institutional level money managers that do just that and just as important, are full disclosure and transparent.

John's Case

Not so for Bob's brother, John. John says he had a $2,000,000 nest egg in 2007 and today it is valued at $1,000,000. He also wants $40,000 annual income for life, but he isn't comfortable with market risk any longer. An idea here would be to split the $1,000,000 into three accounts. The first account (laddered CDs, bonds, conservatively managed accounts or annuities) would generate $40,000 annual income for five years. The second account (laddered CDs or a fixed annuity that grows for 5 years, then pays income for 5 years) would grow safely for the same five year period, then generate for example, $45,000 annual income in years 6-10. And, the third account (a fixed annuity with a lifetime income rider) would grow for ten years at a guaranteed rate (5%-8% for income purposes), then pays a lifetime income stream that cannot be outlived.[12]

Nick's Case

Nick, the third brother, says that he likes a little of what each of his two brothers are doing. So, for Nick, it might be appropriate to split his nest egg into two accounts, the first account being a professionally managed con-

---

12   Guarantees backed by the claims paying ability of the insurer.

servative account for the first ten years and the second account (a fixed annuity with a lifetime income rider) would grow on a guaranteed basis (5%-8%) for income purposes. After ten years, he could turn the second account into a lifetime income stream and manage the remainder of the first bucket knowing that his income is guaranteed for the rest of his life. What is this guaranteed income stream? It is a Lifetime Income Rider that can be attached to many annuities.

Lifetime Income Riders

Lifetime Income Riders are riders that you attach to annuities. The rider guarantees the growth of your money for income purposes at a certain rate.[13] There is an annual fee for this type of rider which range from .60% to .95% annually. Typically, the guaranteed growth rates range from 5% to 8% annually. The rider fee is deducted from the account value, not the income account value, therefore, if you have a 7% rider, your money is truly growing at 7% for income purposes.

Example: Let's say you bought a $100,000 index annuity and attached a 7% lifetime income rider with an annual fee of .60%. Your annuity contract will have two things going on simultaneously, the account value (AV) and the income account value (IAV). The account value is yours to control, withdraw from and the interest is linked to the market with principal protection. Simultaneously, for calculation purposes, you have an IAV that is growing at 7% annually for future income purposes. After 9 years, the IAV value will double to $200,000 for income purposes. The policyholder could turn on the income stream in any year, but from a

---

13   Guarantees backed by the claims paying ability of the insurer.

financial planning standpoint, it may make sense to use this type of account for guaranteed growth of a portion of your assets, to help guarantee income streams for your lifetime and just let the IAV continue to grow at 7% per year until you need the income. There are single and joint payouts as well as level or increasing payments.

You can find these riders on index and variable annuities.[14]

Before you buy an annuity, please seek advice for your particular situation and read the disclosure and/or prospectus carefully. Be informed.

---

14   Guarantees backed by the claims paying ability of the insurer.

Rule #4

Have a Plan When Your Health Fails

Good financial planning requires someone to help you understand the long-term consequences of the decisions that you make today.

To illustrate this point, I would like to share a hypothetical story of the financial landmine that found Donna and Frank (not real people) recently, of which they are navigating day by day.

Donna and Frank were married in an East Texas town eight years ago. She was 58 and he was 68. Life was good for them, they were seemingly healthy, traveled in their RV, visited foreign lands, were members of the local church and active in their community.

After about 5 years of marriage, some symptoms began developing for Donna that were concerning. She couldn't remember certain things, began losing her balance, began falling and fracturing bones and was losing weight.

After three years of these symptoms and many doctor visits, their life was turned upside down when her diagnosis was *progressive supranuclear palsy*. This disease is rare, progressively gets worse, there is no cure and you just manage the symptoms.

Just when it seemed like life was a rose garden for Donna and Frank, this happened. I'll tell you the rest of the story but before I do, let me assure you, this happens all across America every day to boomers and retirees alike.

Other situations may not be as dire as Donna and Frank's reality, but when the day comes that your health fails, what are your plans, financially speaking? How will you pay that first bill? What financial toll would it exact on you and your family?

Today, Donna is in a nursing home in that East Texas town. Frank says that he pays the monthly bill of $6,000 monthly. And, an additional $500 monthly for prescriptions.

That's $6,500 each month or $78,000 each year that Frank will have to pay for Donna to receive the care she currently is getting. In the 15% tax-bracket, that is $91,764 gross annual income that is needed to be able to pay the $78,000 long-term care bill each year.

Neither Donna or Frank have long-term care insurance. They are among the ranks of the "self-insured", which means they are on the hook for 100% of the costs for long-term care services for them both. Frank was overheard describing this financial landmine has him questioning how he will have anything to live on for the remainder of his life.

A study by the U.S. Department of Health and Human Services says that people who reach age 65 will likely have a 40 percent chance of entering a nursing home.[15] About 10 percent of the people who enter a nursing home will stay there five years or more.

---

15   http://www.medicare.gov/longtermcare/static/home.asp

If Donna stays in the nursing home for three years, that is close to $300,000 gross dollars that will be needed for her care during that period.

Are there solutions available that could have helped Donna and Frank from a financial standpoint? Yes.

There are two solutions that I will share with you, that would help protect and preserve your assets when the day comes that you or your spouse may need long-term care services. Before I do, we need to look at Medicare and Medicaid, to learn whether or not the government (taxpayers) will pay for LTC services.

Medicare was not designed to cover ongoing long term care services.

Medicare is the federal medical insurance program for people age 65 or older, and disabled persons of any age receiving Social Security benefits for not less than 24 months. It was designed to pay some of the costs of certain health care services in order to provide recipients access to a basic level of health care. The majority of care provided in the U.S. today in connection with chronic long term illnesses or conditions is personal or custodial care.

Like most health care insurance, Medicare does not pay for custodial care. Medicare only pays for services that are considered "medically necessary" according to Medicare guidelines. This might include a skilled nursing facility and home health care for a period of time as part of treatment of an injury or acute illness, but not on an ongoing basis. One example would be rehabilitation services in a skilled nursing facility as described below.[16]

- Following a hospitalization of at least three days for treatment of a hip fracture, Medicare would pay up to the first 20 days of a stay in a Medicare-certified skilled nursing facility as long as the individual requires skilled services such as nursing and physical therapy prescribed by a physician.

- Days 21 through 100 may be covered if the individual continues to meet Medicare criteria for skilled care. Each of these days would have a co-payment determined yearly by the Centers for Medicare & Medicaid Services (CMS). Medigap policies may cover the daily co-payment amount.

- After 100 days, Medicare will pay nothing for these services. Also, if it is determined that the individual no longer meets Medicare criteria for skilled care prior to 100 days, services will be discontinued. When an individual is receiving Medicare-covered services, regular eligibility reviews are performed to determine ongoing eligibility.

Medigap (also known as **Medicare Supplement Insurance**) includes 12 standard plans (with a few state specific differences) labeled A-L which are defined by Medicare but offered through private insurers. They are intended to cover some of the "gaps" in Medicare.

These gaps include the costs of coinsurance, co-payments, and deductibles. Some of the plans offer benefits not offered through Medicare, such as emergency travel coverage out-

---

16   www.medicare.gov

side of the U.S. Like Medicare, Medigap does not cover on-going long term care services.

Medicaid, under current law, will pay for long-term care services for certain individuals once you prove to the state that you are impoverished.

There are many myths out there, including one rumor that says to qualify for Medicaid, you have to spend-down your assets until you have just a few thousand dollars remaining.

My firm works with many elder law and estate planning attorneys that tell me, that is not necessarily the case. In fact, before you or anyone you know begins to spend-down their assets in an attempt to qualify for Medicaid, contact an elder law attorney in your area for their advice or call my firm and we will put you in touch with a leading elder law firm in Houston to answer your questions.

Let's get back to Donna and Frank.

Other than Medicare and Medicaid, there are two solutions that could have helped Donna and Frank.

It is traditional long-term care insurance and asset-based long term care insurance.

If you become unable to care for yourself because of a prolonged physical illness, a disability, or a cognitive impairment, long-term care services is a type of personal care service you may need.

Long term care services are different from traditional medical care that attempts to treat or cure illnesses. Long-term care helps you maintain your current standard of living, but it generally does not improve or correct your medical problems. Care may be provided at home, in an adult day care center, nursing home, assisted living facility or hospice care.

Long-term care can be expensive. The cost depends on the amount and type of care you need, where you receive it, and what type of medical professional provides it. On average in Texas, it costs about:[17]

- $3,000 per month to live in an assisted living center

- $190 per day for a private room in a nursing home

- $40 a day for adult day care

- $20 a day for a home health aide

To find out how much coverage you might need, call local nursing homes, home health care agencies, and adult day care centers and ask about their cost for daily care. Keep in mind that costs will likely increase as you get older.

Traditional Long Term Care Insurance

Traditional long-term care insurance is a type of insurance developed specifically to cover the costs of long-term care services, most of which are not covered by traditional health insurance or Medicare. This includes services in your home such as assistance with activities of daily living (ADL) as well as care in a variety of facility and community settings.

---

17   http://www.tdi.state.tx.us/pubs/consumer/cb032.html

There is a great deal of choice and flexibility in long-term care insurance policies. You can select a range of care options and benefits that allow you to get the services you need in the settings that suit you best. The cost of your long-term care insurance policy is based on the type and amount of services you choose to have covered, your age when you buy the policy, and any optional benefits you choose. If you are in poor health or already receiving long-term care services, you may not qualify for long-term care insurance.

Long-term care insurance policies have a benefit period or lifetime benefit maximum, which is the total amount of time or total amount of dollars up to which benefits will be paid. Common benefit periods for long-term care policies are two, three, four, and five years.

With traditional long-term care insurance, you pay premiums in amounts you know in advance and can budget for, and the policy pays – up to its coverage limits – for the long-term care you need when you need it. Typically, premiums increase over time and some insurers waive premiums during the time you are receiving benefits.

Policy and Benefit Choices [18]

The following is a summary of policy and benefit choices:

- You select a daily benefit amount (for example, $100 per day), which is the maximum daily amount of expenses for care the policy will pay. Most policies let you choose from $50 per day to as much as $500 per day. A growing number of policies specify benefits

---

18 http://www.longtermcare.gov/LTC/Main_Site/Paying_LTC/Private_Programs/
LTC_Insurance/index.aspx

in terms of a monthly amount so that you have the flexibility to receive more care on some days (for example, when family care is not available) and less care on other days.

- You choose a Maximum Lifetime Benefit you want the policy to provide. Policies typically offer a choice of lifetime dollar amounts – for example $100,000 or $300,000. The dollar amounts may correspond to a period of time.

- Most policies today are comprehensive, but some people prefer to buy facility care only policies. These pay for care in a nursing home or assisted living facility, but not for care at home or in the community. These policies may still include hospice or respite care but only when those services are provided in a facility. Facility-care-only policies cost less than comprehensive policies, and if people prefer and have family or friends to provide care at home, they may only have the policy to reimburse them for paid care in a facility if and when they need it.

- Many policies offer additional optional benefits or "riders" allowing you to customize your coverage. One important option is Inflation Protection, which helps protect you from the rising cost of care over time.

- Most policies offer benefits in a variety of settings, such as your home, an adult day care center, an assisted living community, or a nursing home.

- There are also waiting periods, typically 30, 60, 90 days before the policy will pay benefits. The longer the waiting period, the lower the premium.

For more details on comparing traditional long-term care policies, seek out at least two insurance agents in your area and ask them to help you design the type of policy you want and compare the costs versus the benefits.

The majority of boomers I've met in my career, don't want to purchase the traditional type because if they never need it, according to them, they paid all of those premiums for nothing. I can understand that mindset, however, would that mean that if your house never burned down or you never were involved in an auto accident or never needed long-term care services, then all of those insurance premiums you paid over the years was for naught? It's insurance, you buy it to cover a risk that you hope never happens to you, but are you prepared in the event it does.

However, if that is how you feel, let's discuss an alternative long-term coverage plan that might be just what you are looking for. It's called 'asset-based' long-term care insurance.

Asset-Based Long Term Care Insurance

Asset-based long term care is life insurance and long-term care protection in a single policy, protecting your assets from the risk of long-term care expenses while providing an income tax-free death benefit you can pass to your loved ones. You will have to qualify for this coverage based on your health history.

- **Interest credits and tax-deferred growth**
  Generally, the company guarantees a minimum amount of interest each year and the account value grows tax deferred.

- **Lifetime money back guarantee**
  Some policies will even refund your money, if you fund your policy with a single premium payment and at any time, decide it no longer meets your needs (minus any interest, loans, withdrawals or benefits paid). It is a pretty unique concept.

- **Income tax-free death benefit**
  If you never need long term care services and you never get a return of your premium, then your loved ones will receive the policy's death benefit, income tax-free.

- **Lifetime benefit guarantee**
  The guarantees of all insurance policies are backed by the insurer. Taking loans and withdrawals may jeopardize your policy performance and guarantees, and have tax implications. Each month, the insurance costs for mortality and long-term care coverage are deducted from the account value.

- **Expenses**
  This type of coverage is a life insurance policy with an optional long-term care benefit rider attached. There is a surrender charge schedule, expenses and fees for the life insurance coverage and the long-term care rider. If you are considering this type of policy, please read the illustration, disclosure and brochure carefully.

It is possible to have long term care coverage that will pay if you need it and will pay your heirs a death benefit if you don't. There's also a 100% money-back guarantee if you ever change your mind and want your original premium back. This is possible with an asset-based long term care policy.

To sum up, we've learned that there are four ways to provide long-term care services; Medicare, Medicaid, traditional LTC insurance and Asset-based LTC insurance. Before deciding which type of coverage to apply for, seek counsel from a trusted advisor to help you weigh advantages and disadvantages of each. Be informed.

Rule #5

Avoid These Two Potential Costly IRA Mistakes

In the next few pages you'll learn the full story about IRA investing. You'll learn about two IRA mistakes that have the potential to snare many unsuspecting IRA owners. You will also learn how you may be able to save tens or even hundreds of thousands of dollars in taxes on your IRA over your and your family's lifetime.

Taking a few minutes to read this chapter will help you learn about "the rest of the story" when it comes to your retirement accounts.

Potential IRA Mistake #1:
Believing that continuing to defer taxes inside
of your IRA account indefinitely, is the best
route for your particular situation.

While saving for retirement in an IRA account or 401(k) plan may provide you with tax savings when you make the contribution, there will come a day when the tax bill has to be paid. I'm sure you've heard of what many IRA advocates say:

"Put money away while you're working and receive a tax-deduction today because you're in a high tax-bracket.

Then, when you retire and begin withdrawing money from your IRA, you'll be in a lower tax-bracket and pay less taxes."

How many of us have heard that before? If that was true for everyone that retired, then I wouldn't have written this chapter. But quite often, I have found that this is simply NOT the case.

The longer you allow an investment to accumulate inside an IRA account (provided the account grows), the bigger your tax bill becomes.

As an example, let's look at Ken and Susan (hypothetical purposes only, not real people). Ken worked for years as an engineer with a large aerospace company. He took advantage of his company's 401(k) plan as much as possible through the years. Although the company didn't provide matching contributions, Ken still contributed all that he could to the plan.

By making tax-deductible contributions to a 401(k) plan during his working years, Ken was able to reduce his income tax bill each year. And because the retirement plan grew on a tax-deferred basis, Ken delayed paying the taxes on the growth of the retirement account during those years.

While tax-deferral can provide valuable tax savings, there are individual financial situations in which continued tax-deferral may not be the best financial strategy.

By the time Ken retired, he had accumulated over $400,000 in his 401(k) plan, which he rolled over to an IRA account.

Ken and Susan are withdrawing $2,000 per month from his IRA to supplement their retirement income. Along with their Social Security income, Ken and Susan are getting along nicely during retirement. But, little do they know, in their particular situation, they probably could have gotten along even better from a tax standpoint.

Ken and Susan's tax liability on the $2,000 monthly withdrawals average about $500 per month[19] during their lifetime. Let's also assume that Ken and Susan live 20 years during retirement and their individual income tax rate is 25% for all those years. For illustration purposes, we'll also assume that the IRA balance grows at 10% annually.[20] I know there are a lot of numbers here, but stay with me, I'll make my point quickly.

Based on the above assumptions, the following describes what Ken and Susan's IRA looks like for the 20 years they live during retirement, and what happens when their two children inherit the IRA and elect to take the proceeds in a lump sum.

Ken and Susan pay taxes of $120,000 ($6,000 x 20 yrs = $120,000) during their lifetime and leave an untaxed IRA balance of $1,316,400 to their heirs. We assumed earlier that the heirs would take the IRA balance in a lump-sum, causing them to pay another huge chunk in taxes. It wouldn't be unusual on an IRA balance of over one million dollars to be taxed at the highest individual income tax rate of 35% (as of 2011). The reason is because the heirs would be adding the

---

19   For this example, we're assuming a 25% tax-bracket for life. It should be understood that Congress has the authority to change tax-brackets and tax law as permitted. Early withdrawal penalty applies under age 59 ½ unless you meet an exception.

20   Market-sensitive investments are not FDIC insured, may lose value and are not guaranteed.

inherited dollars on top of their earned income for the year, when they file their tax return. Inherited IRAs do not get a *step-up in basis*[21] like stocks would.

Assuming Ken and Susan's heirs pay all the taxes due at a rate of 35%, they would pay taxes of **$460,740** (35% of $1,316,400), leaving them with **$855,660** to spend or invest. This may sound OK to some folks, but, I say that this mistake may be avoided with proper planning.

And, if Ken and Susan's estate is subject to estate taxes, the tax bill goes even higher.

The total amount paid in taxes on Ken's IRA account during the lifetime of Ken and Susan and at their death is **$604,740**, based on these assumptions.[22] How can anyone pay **$604,740** taxes on a **$400,000** IRA? The answer for Ken and Susan was 20 years of tax-deferral and using the assumptions described earlier.

If a future Congress raises the income tax rates, the total tax bill could be even higher. If, on the other hand, you believe a future Congress will reduce income tax rates, the tax bill could be smaller.

The bottom line is that once you're retired, continuing to accumulate assets in an IRA account may end up costing you and your family 30%-40% in needless income taxes.

---

21   Step-up in basis is the higher market value of an inherited asset on the date of death, not the owners original purchase price.

22   Actual results could vary greatly depending on, but not limited to changes in tax laws, market volatility, actual returns, beneficiary elections, and the affect of inflation on these funds. The tax projection illustrated here assumes zero estate taxes.

An alternative that may benefit the heirs more favorably than a lump sum is a stretch IRA, which allows the inheritor to only withdraw the minimum annual amount based on the inheritor's age, potentially stretching the IRA over many years.

Another alternative is to have the parents purchase a last-to-die life insurance policy and pay for the premiums with IRA dollars. The heirs would inherit the IRA and the life insurance policy (tax-free), of which they could pay the tax bill on the IRA with tax-free dollars.

Seek a trusted advisor to help you determine the most efficient way for you to distribute your retirement accounts, while living and at death.

Potential IRA Mistake #2:
Believing that naming your children as beneficiary
of your IRA account, is a good way to pass
wealth from one generation to the next!

As an example, let's review the financial situation of Margaret (not a real person, for hypothetical purposes only).

Margaret, age 72, has three sons and each is independent and doing fairly well financially. Margaret's wish is for her sons to inherit as much of her assets as possible with minimum government and court interference. Margaret has an IRA account with a balance of **$600,000**.

She is taking only required minimum distributions from her IRA account.[23] Margaret has no need to use her IRA assets for income since she has a relatively modest lifestyle and receives a monthly pension and Social Security check. Margaret's main financial goal is to keep the IRA assets available should she have a large medical bill or need long-term care services. If she doesn't need the IRA assets, she wants them to be distributed to her sons with minimal taxation.

Let's assume the IRA grows at a net rate of 7% annually[24], after Margaret has taken her required minimum distributions from the IRA during her lifetime, and Margaret lives to age 84. Here's what Margaret's situation would look like.

At Margaret's death, the IRA balance is **$715,942** and will pass to her sons who are named as beneficiaries on her IRA account. Let's assume that Margaret's three sons decide to take a lump-sum settlement from the IRA account.[25]

It wouldn't be unusual for Margaret's three sons to pay income taxes at a rate of 35% on the IRA proceeds. The reason is because the heirs would be adding the inheritance dollars on top of their earned income for the year, when they file their tax return.

---

23   The IRS requires that when IRA owners attain age 70 ½, they begin withdrawing money from their IRA account over their life expectancy, until the account is depleted.

24   Actual returns may vary greatly depending on actual investment returns, future changes in tax laws, market volatility, when the account owner dies, and the effect of inflation on these funds.

25   More favorable options other than a lump-sum settlement may be available to a beneficiary, depending on each individual financial situation, actual tax law at the time of inheritance and actual investment returns.

At that tax rate, Margaret's sons would pay total income taxes of **$250,580**, leaving each son with **$155,120** to spend however they want.

The IRS benefits much more than Margaret's children. In fact, the IRS receives almost twice as much as each son.

You can see from this example that IRA accounts have taxes that are owed, at some point, by either you or your heirs.

By now, you're probably sitting there with an IRA account and wondering if you have planned to minimize the taxes that you and your heirs will pay on your IRA accounts during your lifetimes.

Because the tax code has many different rules and different applications of those rules, planning to keep your IRA tax bill at a minimum requires knowledge of your individual financial situation and the consideration of various advanced planning strategies.

Seek out a trusted advisor and become informed.

Rule #6

Get a Basic Estate Plan In Order

In my experience the majority of boomers and retirees I've advised, haven't done any estate planning, or if they have, it was years ago and their documents needed to be reviewed by an attorney for adequacy today. Estate planning is one of those items that you address when you "get around to it".

Your loved ones will be the beneficiaries of the planning that you do today. Often there are bitter and costly family fights after one or both parents die. And, it is usually over small issues or something that could have been avoided, if only the parents had put their wishes in writing and not left it to the children to try and figure out exactly what they wanted to happen.

In this chapter, you'll hear results of an interview I conducted with a Houston area certified estate planning attorney.[26] I asked this attorney 16 of the most common questions that help boomers discern if they need a will , a trust, or nothing at all. Remember, readers should seek tax or legal advice for your particular situation.

1) What is a Will and why should I have one?

A Will is a written document in which you direct disposition of your property following your death.

---

26   Dean Shearer, certified estate planning attorney, Houston, TXs.

Advantages of a Will:

- *You* determine who inherits your property (not a Judge) and any alternate beneficiaries.

- *You* select Executor of your estate and Guardian of minor children (not a Judge).

- More efficient administration of your estate, resulting in reduced probate costs and delays.

- Reduced death taxes with proper planning.

Do you have a Will? If so, when was it last reviewed?

2) What property passes under my Will?

Non-probate Assets - life insurance proceeds, joint tenancy with right of survivorship accounts, and death benefits under retirement plans generally do *not* pass under your Will.

Probate Assets - generally everything else passes under your Will, such as jewelry, collectibles, house, car, etc.

Who are the beneficiaries of your life insurance and retirement plans? Do you have any JTWROS property?

3) Who is my Executor?

An "Executor", or the feminine gender "Executrix", is the person appointed in your Will to wind up your affairs (An "Administrator" is appointed by the Judge to carry out these duties if you have no Will).

Who is named as Executor in your Will? Alternates?

4) Who will be my child's Guardian?

a. A *Guardian of the Person* has custody and the responsibility for the physical care of a minor during the period of guardianship.

b. A *Guardian of the Estate* is responsible for the Ward's assets during the guardianship. (This expensive and cumbersome process can be avoided by using a trust.)

Who would you want as guardian for your children?

5) What is Probate?

Probate is the process of proving your Will is valid and appointing a "personal representative" (Executor or Administrator) for the purpose of terminating your affairs. Probate administration requires the Executor to locate your assets, file an Inventory with the probate court listing those assets, pay your debts, taxes and estate expenses, and distribute the remaining assets to those beneficiaries named in your Will. If there is no Will, your estate is left to your heirs as determined under state law.

- *Dependent Probate Administration* - in most states, including Texas, virtually all of the Executor's duties and actions are subject to advance approval by probate court, which is an expensive and time consuming process.

- *Independent Probate Administration* - Texas law allows you to appoint an "Independent Executor" in your

Will , to act independently of control by Texas probate court, except for filing of the required Inventory.

Does your Will allow for Independent Administration under Texas law?

6) What happens if I die without a Will?

- A judge appoints an Administrator, who must post a bond, and act subject to "Dependent" Probate Administration, which is an expensive and time consuming process.

- An heirship hearing must be held to determine identity of "heirs" under state law.

Will your estate be subject to unnecessary additional expense, delay and uncertainty because you don't have a will?

7) Who are my "Heirs" ?

It depends. Your spouse may not inherit everything if there is "separate property" involved or if there are children from a prior marriage. If you have no spouse or children, then basically your "next-of-kin" will inherit.

Who would inherit your estate (by Will or by law)?

8) What is Community Property in Texas?

- *Community Property* – This is all other property acquired during marriage which includes salary and income earned from separate property assets. Each spouse owns an undivided one-half.

- *Separate Property* – This is all property acquired before marriage or acquired in another state during marriage which is not community property under the law of that state. Property received at any time by gift or inheritance, or acquired at any time by separate property funds.

If married, do you know what is community and what is separate property?

---

9) What is a Trust?

A Trust is created when you (as the *Trustor, Grantor, or Settlor)* transfer legal ownership of property to another person or corporation (the *Trustee)* to be held for the benefit of yourself or another (the *Beneficiary).*

- A Trust created during your lifetime is called an *inter-vivos* or *Living Trust.*

- An *irrevocable trust* is one which cannot be modified or dissolved by you as Trustor and typically used to avoid death taxes. When you as Trustor retain the right to modify or dissolve the trust, it is a *revocable trust* and is typically used for probate avoidance.

- A Trust created under your Will is called a *testamentary trust* and does not come into existence until *after* your death, at which time the trust becomes irrevocable. Testamentary trusts may be used to save death taxes, to provide for a spouse's lifetime needs, while preserving the remainder for children, or to defer distribution of an inheritance until a child is of legal age or is financially and emotionally mature.

Is a testamentary trust appropriate for your Will?

10) Who is my Trustee?

A Trustee is the person responsible for administration of your trust estate, whether the trust is created under a Will or during your lifetime. The Trustee is responsible for prudently investing the trust assets and making distributions of trust income and principal to the beneficiary within the guidelines established in the instrument creating the trust.

Who would you name as Trustee?

11) Why use a revocable Living Trust?

- Advantages - avoids expenses and delays associated with probate of a Will, avoids ancillary probate for out-of-state real property, insures privacy; provides asset management for a disability.

- Disadvantages - more complicated and expensive to create than a Will; still need a Will; assets must be transferred into a trust during lifetime to avoid probate.

Is a revocable Living Trust appropriate for you?

12) What are Death Taxes and when do they apply?

Federal *estate* and state *inheritance* taxes are excise taxes on the right to transfer property at death or the right to inherit. An *unlimited* amount may pass to a U.S. citizen spouse or charity without being subject to estate tax.

Estates passing to anyone other than a spouse or charity in excess of the "Exclusion Amount" are subject to estate tax. The new tax law passed December 17, 2010 increased the Exclusion Amount to $5,000,000 per individual and decreased the tax rate to 35% for 2011 and 2012.

Unfortunately, the Exclusion Amount reverts back to $1,000,000 with a 55% top rate in 2013, unless Congress makes further changes in the law. Federal *gift tax* also applies for certain gifts in excess of $13,000 per donee annually, in addition to the lifetime Exclusion Amount.

A *generation skipping transfer tax* also may apply. (Techniques for reducing or eliminating these taxes are beyond the scope of this discussion.)

Are death taxes a concern for you?

13) I am not wealthy, so do I still need a Will?

You need a Will if you are:

- Single, no children

- Single, with children

- Married, no children

- Married with children

- Second marriage, with or without children (his/hers/their kids)

f. Non-traditional relationship (unmarried life partners)...

Who do you want to inherit under your personal circumstances?

14) If I already have a Will, when should it be reviewed?

Your Will and other estate planning documents should not be put away and forgotten until it is too late to change them (after death or disability has occurred). These important documents should be reviewed periodically, and revised to reflect changed circumstances.

- Birth of a child or grandchild.

- Death of a beneficiary (spouse, child or grandchild) or fiduciary (Executor or Trustee).

- Marriage or remarriage of yourself or a beneficiary.

- Divorce of yourself or a beneficiary.

- Change in wealth.

- Purchase of additional life insurance.

- Purchase or sale of a business.

- Move to or from another state.

- Retirement or pending retirement.

- Changes in federal or state tax or property laws.

Have there been any changes in your circumstances since you last reviewed your Will?

15) What is a Power of Attorney?

A court created guardianship may be necessary to appoint a guardian for you if you become disabled. A Power of Attorney allows you (as the Principal) to designate a legal representative (Agent) to act on your behalf if you are physically or mentally incapable of doing so.

- *General Durable Power of Attorney* - to handle legal and financial matters.

- *Health Care Power of Attorney* - to make health care decisions.

Do you have a Power of Attorney?

16) What are the advantages of estate planning?

- The ability to choose your beneficiaries, as well as the amount and timing of distributions.

- Select the Executor/Trustee/Guardian.

- Reduce probate expense and delays.

- Reduce death taxes.

- Provide incapacity planning for asset management during your lifetime.

Have you left a well planned estate for your family? When you walk out on life, do you have continuity in your plan so that everything happens just the way you want? If you have uncertainties or concerns regarding your estate planning (or lack thereof), seek counsel from an estate planning attorney to review your particular situation. Be informed.

Rule #7

Know the Difference Between a Broker and an Advisor.

Wikipedia.com and Merriam-Webster Dictionary defines a *broker* as one who sells or distributes something and is paid a commission when the deal is executed. An advisor is defined as someone that gives you a recommendation about your options.

My definition of a *broker* is someone that works at a brokerage firm and sells investment products for that firm. The broker isn't required to put the clients' interests first. He or she is only required to make 'suitable' recommendations, which may not necessarily be the 'best' recommendations.

My definition of an *advisor* is someone you would expect to pay a fee for their advice and then decide whether or not to implement their advice. An advisor is required to act as a fiduciary, which is always acting in the clients' best interests.

The Wall Street Journal ran an article[27] in December 2010 regarding brokers. Here is an excerpt;

"There's no question that the average client perceives his broker at a large wirehouse in the same way he perceives his doctor, lawyer or CPA," says Andrew Stoltmann, a Chicago-based securities lawyer who represents investors in disputes against

---

27 *The Wall Street Journal*, Suzanne Barlyn, December 6, 2010

brokerage firms. *"People assume their brokers are always looking out for their best interests."*

Many brokers may, in fact, look out for their clients' best interests. But if they're not registered as investment advisers in addition to being registered as brokers, they're not legally obligated to meet that standard.

Barbara Roper, investor-protection director for the Consumer Federation of America, a Washington-based advocacy group says, *"brokers typically are paid through commissions, which can complicate the relationship. Also, brokerage firms may earn fees from investment companies for promoting their products, such as certain mutual funds. The broker is free to recommend inferior options that compensate the broker more generously, rather than what's best for the investor. They may take their firm's interests into account, as well."*

Now that you know the difference between a broker and advisor, it is not my intent to lump all brokers or advisors in the same mold. I'm sure there are some brokers that act in their clients best interests as I'm sure there are some advisors that don't always put their clients' interest first. As we all know, there will always be a few bad apples in each basket.

When searching for financial advice, my recommendation would be to interview a couple of advisors, select one, pay the fee for their objective advice, go through their consultation meetings, become informed and then decide whether or not you are comfortable with this person and if you want to implement the plan they design for you.

At least when you pay a planning fee, you tend to get more of an objective view and you are always in control. If you don't like the plan, you can have the advisor tweak it or you can walk away altogether. You receive professional advice and the adviser is paid for his time.

Be informed.

About the Author

Jim E. Sloan is a wealth manager and president of Jim Sloan & Associates, an estate and retirement planning firm with offices in Friendswood, Texas and the Houston Galleria area. Mr. Sloan is an Investment Advisor Representative of Global Financial Private Capital, LLC, an SEC Registered Investment Advisor. This relationship allows Jim Sloan & Associates to bring institutional level experience, practices and pricing to individuals and business owners age 55 and better. Mr. Sloan is supported by an administrative staff, a financial planning team, CPAs, estate planning and elder law attorneys, to help clients achieve their financial and re-tirement goals.

Mr. Sloan also authored a book titled *How To Avoid Huge IRA Tax-Traps*, published in 2006. He publishes a quarterly newsletter *The Financial Times*, regularly writes timely con-sumer reports and conducts private and public speaking engagements, discussing the ever-changing economic and financial landscape, as well as the opportunities that these changes bring.

In 2009, 2010 and 2011, Mr. Sloan was recognized as a "FIVE STAR Wealth Manager" for overall client satisfaction. This distinction represents less than 2% of wealth managers in the Houston Region and is only awarded to wealth manag-ers who have scored highest in a consumer survey under the direction of Crescendo Business Services. Financial pro-fessionals are not able to "buy" their way onto the list and the distinction is based on how consumers have evaluated their experience in working with that individual.

Jim Sloan & Associates believes in a compensation model of transparency and full disclosure, earning fees and commissions for his firm's services. This compensation model allows Mr. Sloan to provide a diverse array of savings, insurance and investment options to solve many problems investors face today.

Mr. Sloan believes that sound retirement planning requires someone helping you understand the long-term consequences of the decisions that you make today. If you are an individual or business owner age 55 or better, Mr. Sloan offers you a *Complimentary Second Opinion* on your current financial path.

Mr. Sloan and his wife, Lorri, reside in Friendswood, believe in the name of Jesus Christ, travel often, play golf together and give back to the less fortunate in their community.

9 780983 728009